CHOPPERS

AND CUSTOM MOTORCYCLES

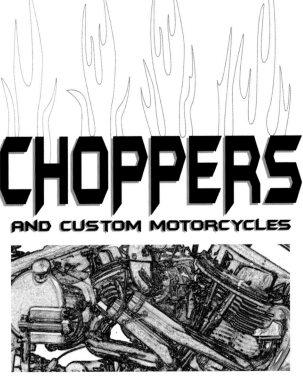

Doug Mitchel

Publications International, Ltd.

CONTENTS

INTRODUCTION

They had once been the province of a small cadre of enthusiasts, but choppers have once hit the big time. Thanks in large part to exposure on national television and cable shows, their combination of sight and sound has made them the equivalent of mobile celebrities.

But choppers as a breed are really not new. In fact, they can trace their heritage to the late 1940s, when surplus military bikes were stripped of unnecessary parts and given homemade paint jobs to become "Bobbers." Bikes sprouting extended forks, stepped saddles, tall sissy bars, and wild paint schemes appeared in the late '60s as "Choppers," and the die was cast.

Today, choppers take many different forms. *Old School* bikes favor the minimalist styling of Bobbers, *Early Choppers* the look of their original namesakes. *Factory* and *Factory-Modified* customs from relatively small companies can be purchased right off the showroom floor, while *Radicals* are ornate rides that can take many months—and dollars—to build. *Pro Street* bikes lean toward performance, and choppers that fall through the categorical cracks can be termed *Special Construction*. In some cases, bikes employ traits of more than one class, making them difficult to place—though we've done it anyway.

As do many fields of interest, the world of choppers contains its own lingo. In the back of this book is a glossary that defines and explains many of the unique terms used to describe the breed. Even if you're familiar with motorcycles—and particularly if you're not—a quick scan of the glossary might help clarify some of the words and descriptions found in these pages.

Many books and television shows have highlighted bikes from the big-name, high-volume builders. What's focused on here are choppers built by lesser-known but equally talented shops and individuals, most of whom produce only a handful of machines a year—and often come up with truly fascinating creations. These bikes provide a look not only at where the chopper phenomenon came from, but also where it's heading. We hope you enjoy the trip.

Captain America

It's perhaps the best-known chopper in the world, and to many, the Captain America bike from the film *Easy Rider* defines the breed.

The bike shown is not a replica; it is one of two identical choppers originally built by Cliff Vaughn for use in *Easy Rider*. This is the one that was wrecked at the end of the film. The other was reportedly stolen, likely sold for parts by a thief unaware of its significance.

After the filming, the wrecked bike was procured by actor Dan Haggerty, who began rebuilding it but never finished. It was then sold, the restoration being completed by Dave Ohrt. The owner, who wishes to remain anonymous, has graciously loaned

Easy Rider, *starring
Dennis Hopper (left)
and Peter Fonda
(driving the Captain
America bike), was
released in 1969, and
soon became a cult
classic.*

it to the National Motorcycle Museum
in Anamosa, Iowa, where it is currently
on display.

This example of the Captain
America bike started life as a 1951
Harley- Davidson FL. The frame was
chromed but is otherwise virtually
stock. So is the engine. Added were
extended forks, ape-hanger handlebars, upswept fishtail mufflers,
"peanut" gas tank, and tall sissy
bar, all of which grew to define
an early chopper.

FLH

year: 1958
builder: Jerry Morgan
class: Early Chopper

Aside from a cherry Early Chopper, what we see here is a study in perseverance; owner Jerry Morgan first customized this 1958 Harley-Davidson FLH in 1969, and has redone it five times since.

In 1971, after undergoing a second "build," the bike was wrecked almost beyond repair. But repair it Jerry did—making it even better than it was before. And that's been the story with each overhaul that has brought it to this, its sixth incarnation.

By now, there is little left of the original 1958 Harley. The frame has been converted to a hardtail configuration, the forks exchanged for an extended girder setup. The engine, while still true to its Panhead design, has been modified for added power and durability; chief among its revisions are a Weber two-barrel carburetor and Alphabet headers. A custom-made fuel tank and classic Invader wheels substitute for the original pieces.

Most obvious among the alterations, however, is the contemporary "chameleon" paint, which looks purple, blue, or green, depending on the angle of view. It represents one of the many improvements made to the bike since its first round of customization back in 1969. And while it appears to have finally reached perfection, one wonders if it's truly "finished."

Although assembled using a lot of Harley-Davidson components, this bike was never a complete Harley to begin with. For one thing, the builder wanted certain features the Milwaukee company never offered to the public.

Primary among those features were the front and rear suspension systems. Hardtail frames were the traditional choice, but they were uncomfortable over bumps. So a Jammer frame was chosen that incorporated a plunger-type rear suspension—similar to that used on old Indian motorcycles—providing a bit of cushioned wheel travel. In front, girder forks have a one-piece design, but move up and down on pivoting links.

Harley-Davidson did, however, supply the drivetrain: a 74-cubic-inch "Shovelhead" V-twin and 4-speed transmission. A two-into-one header from Cycle Shack helps the old engine breathe. Power routes to a stock Harley spoke wheel with drum brake; in front, a Hallcraft 21-inch spoke wheel with disc brake was chosen for more of a "chopper" look.

The fuel tank is set back on the frame's top tube, allowing space for a graphics panel carrying the bike's Mississippi Queen moniker. A set of nearly flat drag bars in tandem with a deeply contoured "King and Queen" seat add an appropriate look to a bike built in the Early Chopper style—which was something never offered by the folks from Milwaukee.

13

Tramp

year: 2004
builder: David Buerer
class: Old School

David Buerer has never been accused of being timid, so when he set out to build his own radical Old School chopper, nothing was considered out of bounds.

A Daytec hardtail frame holds lengthy 32-inch-over telescopic forks at a radical 54-degree rake; you don't need to look at the photos to tell that results in a pretty wild profile. Sixty-spoke wheels were used on both axles, as were disc brakes by Performance Machine.

Powering the Tramp is a V-twin made from aftermarket parts but built to resemble a classic Harley-Davidson Shovelhead engine. It displaces a healthy 93 cubic inches and wears a pair of exhaust pipes bent by Dave himself.

A fuel tank from Mid-USA was stretched to fit the frame's unusual dimensions, and painted matte black to fit David's unusual vision. And the way Tramp turned out, nobody can say that vision was too timid.

EL
year: 1947
builder: Psycle Barn/Rodney Mann/Robert Berry
class: Old School

As a prime example of the Old School chopper, Robert Berry's bike shuns the normal sculpted metal, billet trim, and big-inch engine of most customs, relying instead on a bare-bones look and hardware with historical significance.

Chief among these is the engine: a tried-and-true 74-cubic-inch Harley-Davidson Knucklehead, which is all stock save for the turned-up Paughco exhaust system. Granted, the frame is a modern item—a Paughco with -inch downtube stretch—but the springer forks are very close to those that supported Harleys in the early postwar years.

Of course, this wouldn't be much of a custom without a few nonstock components, but most are anchored in tradition. The fuel tank carries the classic teardrop shape, the rear fender is a cut-down version of the original Harley piece, and the overall look pays homage to 1950s bobbers. Choppers of the 1960s and 1970s inspired the ape-hanger handlebars, a common item on many great Old School bikes.

Above: *You can't get more classic in the powerplant department than a Harley-Davidson Knucklehead. That's not Harley's term for it; the nickname was coined by riders, because the large bolts on the valve covers look like knuckles on a fist.* **Below:** *The original Harley drum brake may suffice up front, but the rear wheel hosts a modern disc.*

Model U

year: 1941
builder: Robert Berry
class: Old School

Harley's classic tank-mounted instrument panel originated in the 1930s. The basic design is still used today, but many feel the old ones were more stylish.

Unlike some Old School choppers, this one really *is* old—with a few exceptions.

A restored-to-stock 1941 Harley-Davidson flathead would be a valuable piece, but Robert Berry is a chopper guy. And he wanted to add a flathead to his stable to keep his chopped 1947 Harley Knucklehead company.

A 1941 Harley-Davidson Model U formed the basis for his flathead chopper. For the most part, the original hardware was retained: a low-compression 74-cubic-inch V-twin, four-speed transmission, hardtail frame, springer forks, and solo saddle with sprung seat post. While a modern hand-clutch/foot-shift arrangement replaces the original foot clutch/hand shift, stock Harley drum brakes are used front and rear, each supporting classic spoked rims.

From there, customization followed a Bobber theme. The fuel tank was modified to hold gas in the left half, oil in the right, thus eliminating the separate oil tank beneath the seat. The front fender is a mere sliver of its former self, and the trimmed rear fender hosts a 1950s-era custom taillight. Only the TT-style exhaust with its tapered-cone mufflers and the artful scalloped paint treatment give this away as a modern machine—because old-time Bobbers never looked this good.

The Hobo is aptly named, as its assorted bits and pieces were collected from many sources over a two-year period. All the adopted parts, which include Schwinn bicycle handgrips and a throttle from a jet ski, were assembled with only a rough idea of the desired outcome; many others, such as the fender brackets and handlebars, were handmade by the builder.

Seated on top of the hardtail frame is a chromed

Shift knob lends a whole new meaning to the phrase "tap it into gear."

Moon fuel tank. Forks are standard Harley-Davidson telescopics, but they carry no headlight; instead, it's mounted low on the left side of the frame, just ahead of the replica Panhead engine, which exhales through stubby handmade pipes. Gears are stirred by a hand shifter topped with a beer-tap handle borrowed from a local saloon. Both footpegs, along with the kick-start pedal, came from a bicycle. One of the few off-the-shelf chopper components is a rear sprocket/brake rotor from the Exile catalog.

While most choppers originate with a design and are then assembled with specific components, The Hobo materialized in a rather different manner. But while the end result may not have been envisioned from the start, if the intent was to build something completely different, then The Hobo came out exactly according to plan.

PURPLE HAZE

year: 1996
builder: Michael Bailey
class: Special Construction

Though first purchased by Michael Bailey in 1974, it was more than 20 years before his 1955 Harley-Davidson would get the chopper treatment. Instead of hiring the work out, he took on the task himself—which resulted in a two-year build time.

A stretched Atlas hardtail frame was substituted for the original, providing a leaner look and more-radical profile. Girder forks replaced the heavy Hydra-Glide telescopics, and modern wheels and brakes were fitted at each end.

Displacement of the original Panhead V-twin remains at 74 cubic inches, but many parts have been replaced with modern, high-performance substitutes. The "Who's Who" list of internal hardware includes a Sifton cam, STD heads, S&S crank, and Wiseco pistons. A single SU carburetor tends the fuel mixture, which is lit by a Mallory ignition.

To complete his first project bike, Michael applied blue-to-red chameleon paint to every square inch of steel. A Harley-Davidson logo dresses the fuel tank, and a layer of chrome dresses the oil tank and forks.

It may have taken two decades for Michael to convert his old Harley into a stunning chopper, but judging from the outcome, it was worth the wait.

ASTROZOMBIE

year: 2005
builder: Jason Hart/Chopsmith
class: Special Construction

If you spend any time around Jason Hart of Chopsmiths, you soon realize the word "stock" is simply not part of his bike-building vocabulary. Any time he sets his sights on building another chopper, very few off-the-shelf components will be used—and most of those will be modified.

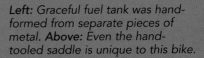

Left: *Graceful fuel tank was hand-formed from separate pieces of metal.* **Above:** *Even the hand-tooled saddle is unique to this bike.*

A frame from RC Components was the starting point for Astrozombie, but—not surprisingly—it was tweaked a bit for this application. So were the Harley-Davidson Deuce forks. A Harley Shovelhead engine enlarged to 93 cubic inches provides plenty of motivational force.

The exotic contours of the rear fender, fuel tank, and side plates all began life as flat sheets of metal; Jason hand-formed, polished, and finished them with the help of his son, Devan.

Despite the wide variety of lights available in the aftermarket, Jason wanted to make his own. The headlight is fashioned out of a piston from a Cummins diesel engine, the taillight from an early Ford stop-lamp. So it can rightfully be said that, from head to tail, the Astrozombie is truly a custom-built machine.

year: 2004
builder: American IronHorse
class: Factory

"Real flame" paint's soft edges make the fire look more... well...real. Eyebrow gauge panel just ahead of the forks holds a digital speedometer and bar-graph tachometer.

Of all the bikes American IronHorse builds, the Texas Chopper displays the most extreme geometry and appearance. Lengthy chrome forks are mated with a stretched fuel tank that reaches all the way back to the seat. The choice of "real flame" paint only adds to the radical look. Power for this example comes from a 117-cubic-inch S&S V-twin; it's the midsized engine offered for this model, the others displacing 111 and 124 cubic inches. All Texas Choppers come with a 6-speed gearbox regardless of powerplant.

In addition to a wide choice of colors and graphics, American IronHorse offers a selection of 12 different wheel styles. The Gladiator pattern was chosen for this model, and as with all AIH machines, the wheels, drive pulley, and brake rotors are cut in the same design. Extensive use of polished billet pieces makes this stand-out machine stand out even more.

27

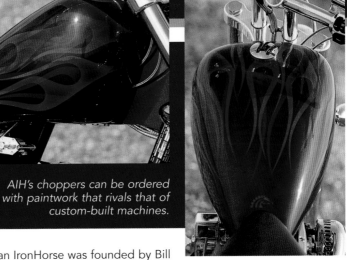

AIH's choppers can be ordered with paintwork that rivals that of custom-built machines.

American IronHorse was founded by Bill Rucker and Tim Edmondson in 1995. Since then, the company has grown into one of the country's largest producers of "factory" choppers. Model offerings range from mild to wild, with the lineup growing every year.

The Legend is one of the more traditional models in AIH's line, but is still quite innovative. The frame, formed from large-diameter tubing, features a four-inch stretch and a triangulated-swingarm rear suspension. Forks are stretched six inches and mounted at a 38-degree rake. Wheels, brake rotors, and the drive pulley share the same design, and four-piston brake calipers are used on both wheels. A 21-inch tire is mounted up front, a 240-mm 18-incher in back. AIH produces its own saddles, and every Legend comes complete with an electronic digital instrument cluster.

A 107-cubic-inch S&S engine is the base powerplant, but larger 117- and 124-inch options can be ordered. The two-into-one exhaust by AIH extracts more power from the engine than traditional (for a chopper, anyway) two-into-two designs.

American IronHorse sells a number of different motorcycles in a variety of designs through more than 100 dealers in the United States. Each bike can be customized with a selection of wheels and colors.

The basis for the LSC is a hardtail frame with 4-inch stretch, 8-inch rise, and 38-degree rake in the neck. Triple trees add another four degrees, for a total of 42 degrees of fork rake. Forks are 12-inch-over telescopics, and combine with the tall frame for an extreme stance. A 124-cubic-inch S&S engine is fitted to this example, but 107- and 113-cubic-inch versions are also available. The 6-speed transmission has right-side belt drive.

The wheels shown are AIH's Lonestars; their design is echoed in the brake rotors and drive pulley. Two features of the LSC not found on many choppers are the strutless rear fender, which provides a cleaner appearance, and dual front brakes for better stopping power.

Bourget's Bike Works (BBW) has been building extreme machines for many years, and one of its more radical designs is the Retro Chopper. By melding the apparent fuel tank and frame members into a single component, Bourget's achieves an unusually unified look.

It's an "apparent" fuel tank because the formed metal serves as little more than a broad canvas for applied graphics; in this case, the stars of a "Stars and Stripes" theme. Fuel and oil are carried within the frame tubes.

The 47-degree rake and 18-inch stretch of the springer forks make for a radical front end. Equally notable is the tail, which incorporates a labyrinth of tubing, but no suspension.

A 113-cubic-inch S&S engine sends power to a 280-series tire mounted on a BBW wheel that mimics the four-spoke "mag" style of the front rim. The rear axle rides in a machined tailpiece that also hosts the brake caliper.

Making this chopper stand out even more is its red, white, and blue paint scheme—as if this extreme machine needed to attract any more attention....

DropSeat 280

DD Customs is a relatively new player in the high-end chopper arena, but its creations exhibit a level of detail and creativity usually associated with experienced builders.

The DropSeat 280 model features a chassis from War Eagle that rolls on a 280-series rear tire. The Tricky Air rear suspension provides complete control over ride height and firmness. War Eagle forks are canted at a 42-degree rake and cut down two inches from stock dimensions. Pro-One wheels were given a red anodized finish that contrasts with their chrome "star" accents. A fuel tank from Independent was extensively reworked for the application. Power comes from a 124-cubic-inch S&S engine, the motive force counteracted by HHI disc brakes at each end.

Subtle Silver Candy paint seems to glow in the light, and is accented with Von Dutch-style striping. It all results in an exceptional bike with a unique look that does the newcomers at DD Customs proud.

Glowing Silver Candy paint is set off by the type of free-form pinstriping popularized by artist Von Dutch in the 1960s.

CREEP SHOW

Crown Custom Cycle Fabrication (CCCF) has forged a reputation for high-performance machinery, but can also build bikes with as much "show" as "go." And Creep Show is one of them.

Added to a Bourget's Bike Works frame was a set of 6-inch-over Progressive telescopic forks set at a 42-degree rake. Weld Wheels carrying JB disc brakes hold up both ends. Providing power is a 113-cubic-inch engine from TP Engineering.

Nearly every junction in the hardtail frame has been molded smooth, including those on the fabricated brace for the rear fender. But perhaps the most striking visual element is the "chameleon" paint, which flips from purple to blue to green depending on the angle of view. Static display on a page fails to do the paint job justice, but what does are the numerous trophies picked up at major cycle events—proving this bike really is for "show" as much as for "go."

American Performance Cycles produces a variety of models, and the High Roller 280 RHD is its top-of-the-line machine. Nevertheless, some buyers prefer to take it a step or two beyond.

In addition to his passion for choppers, owner Kevin Murphy has an equally avid love for guitars. Blending the two interests produced the creation shown here.

The starting point was an APC frame with 4-inch stretch, 7-inch rise, and Soft-Ride rear suspension. Ten-inch-over inverted forks are raked at 38 degrees. A 124-cubic-inch S&S engine combines with a 6-speed transmission to add "go" to the "show."

Every piece of sheetmetal is painted in a guitar motif, but there are several other custom touches as well, including an artful kickstand and a taillight set into the trailing edge of the rear fender. Together, they help make this bike a very high roller indeed.

Note the engraving on the kickstand. But the paint job is what really sets a machine apart, and this guitar theme—based on the drawings of a twelfth-century Japanese monk—does the trick.

Aggression

year: 2005
builder: Midwest Choppers
class: Radical

Aggression got off to a rocky start. Begun as a customer order that fell through, Chip Miyler at Midwest Customs decided to complete the project on his own.

A swingarm frame with rear suspension by Progressive mounts 8-inches-over inverted forks at a 51-degree rake. Extreme Machine wheels at both ends feature fine detailing. In front, the brake rotor matches the wheel design; in back, the pulley—which overlays the brake rotor—does the same.

Power comes from a 124-cubic-inch S&S engine polished to a show finish. Air enters through a Midwest Choppers air cleaner, exiting via a Martin Bros. exhaust system.

Elaborate metalwork features a silver spine running from front fender to rear, bisecting the deep purple paint. An aggressive scoop is formed into the base of the frame's downtube, while both fenders wrap deeply around the tires.

As it turned out, six months of toil were required to complete the build, but a Best Radical Custom trophy at a show in Indianapolis made it all worthwhile. Aggression may have started on a low note, but certainly finished on a high one.

Bad Moon

year: 2003
builder: Kenny Rollins/ Chopper Shop, Inc.
class: Radical

Not only is the owner of this bizarre machine responsible for its design, he's also responsible for its creation.

Kenny Rollins built Bad Moon around a hardtail chassis from Killer Choppers, setting a springer fork from the Paughco catalog at a 49-degree rake. The 40-spoke front wheel has a single disc brake, and the Rader mag-style rear wheel is equipped with a combination brake disc/sprocket from Exile.

In between sits an 88-cubic-inch Rev Tech V-twin that combines the look of a vintage Harley-Davidson Panhead engine with the advantages of modern technology. The snakey exhaust system was custom-made by Rollins. A 5-speed Rev Tech transmission gets both hand- and foot-operated shifters.

Perhaps the most obvious design feature is the oversized Moon fuel tank. Coated in chrome, it is mounted directly to the upper frame tube. Other custom touches include a chromed, oval oil tank below the sprung saddle, and a tall, warped sissy bar. It all combines to create a very unusual machine, which is exactly what the owner wanted—and built.

Moon fuel tanks were popular on hot rods and dragsters of the '50s and '60s. A mere accessory on those vehicles, it takes center stage here. The tall Hurst shift lever beside it is another automotive icon of the 1960s.

Beneath the hot-rod-style pleated seat resides an oval oil tank with diamond-plate end caps.

El Balla

year: 2004
builder: Johnny Legend Customs
class: Radical

John Dodson's racing experience and passion for fast motorcycles led to the creation of this, his first custom chopper. It also led to the creation of his company, Johnny Legend Customs.

An RC Components frame hosts American inverted forks raked at 48 degrees. Also from RC Components came a single-sided swingarm and combination brake disc/drive pulley that allow a clear view of the right side of the rear wheel. The front wheel and brake were also supplied by RC Components. Rear air suspension provides an adjustable ride height, allowing the bike to be lowered for "show" and raised for "go."

And go it does, thanks to a 124-cubic-inch V-twin from Total Performance. Pipes from Sampson complete the picture.

Custom-formed bodywork accents the frame and encloses the oil tank. But the focal point is the rear fender, which encapsulates a taillight between staggered layers of sheet-metal. Of course, some might argue the orange and purple paint scheme is what first draws the eye, but either way, it's obvious Johnny Legend Customs is off to a great start.

Spoon Cobra

year: 2004
builder: Fearless Choppers
class: Radical

Martin Dring of Fearless Choppers and Russ Austin of Precious Metal Customs combined their considerable talents to build the Spoon Cobra. With its sculpted sheetmetal and distinctive touches, it was obviously a successful venture.

Beginning with a Precious Metal Customs chassis with 6-inch rise and 5-inch stretch, a 52-degree rake was applied to 24-inch-over forks from Mean Street. Weld wheels were used front and rear, both fitted with Hawg Halter disc brakes. A 280-series rear tire receives power from a 96-cubic-inch S&S engine via a Baker 5-speed transmission with right-side drive.

Every inch of sheetmetal was hand-formed by Fearless Choppers and Precious Metal Customs, creating a truly individual machine. Candy Brandywine paint is highlighted with subtle images, the largest of which covers the top of the concave-sided fuel tank. The end result is a radical chopper that clearly shows what these combined forces can achieve.

Spoon

year: 2005
builder: Precious Metal Customs
class: Radical

Image from rearview camera is displayed on a video screen frenched into the top of the fuel tank.

Machined accents dress the cylinders, primary-drive cover, and frame down-tube. Spire-topped foot-pegs and control pedals follow a theme carried throughout the bike.

Precious Metal Customs, formed in 1998, builds only radical machines, with most pieces being custom-made. For instance, whereas most manufacturers buy frames and sheetmetal off the shelf, PMC creates its own.

The Spoon rides a hardtail chassis carrying a 100-cubic-inch Harley-Davidson engine fitted with Rev Tech internal hardware. Among the bike's unusual features is a rearview camera and video screen that substitute for rearview mirrors—eliminating their often tacked-on look—while allowing the rider a clear view of what he's leaving behind.

Street Hustler

year: 2004
builder: Kaotic Customs
class: Radical

Building cookie-cutter, look-alike choppers is not what Kaotic Customs is all about. Every one of the company's machines is different from the last, the only constant being the pursuit of quality.

Street Hustler is built with hand-formed sheetmetal and custom-made handlebars carrying a sole instrument. The RC Components frame has a 38-degree rake in the neck, with another six degrees added by the triple trees for a total of 44 degrees. Adjustable air suspension acts on a triangulated swingarm at the rear to provide a comfortable ride. RC Components also sourced both the wheels and disc brakes. Power comes from a 113-cubic-inch S&S engine.

It's difficult to categorize the paint scheme other than to say it defies convention. While the upper half of the bike seems cloaked in armor, the bottom half reflects a woodgrain theme. But it matches perfectly Kaotic Customs' creed that no two bikes look alike.

For Pain
Erickson,
not just any
chopper would do.
Thinking others might feel
the same, he decided to build
a series of bikes that met his own exacting
standards.

One was this Candy Red Suicide Softail.
As the name implies, it features a uniquely
styled rear swingarm with adjustable air-

spring
suspension
mounted
behind the engine.
And what an engine it is:
145 cubic inches of V-twin power, with
custom-bent exhaust pipes wrapped in
heat-shielding tape. A 6-speed Baker transmission with hand shifter feeds the ponies
to a combination sprocket/rear brake
affixed to a solid, chromed rear wheel.

year: 2004
builder: Thee Darkside of Daytona
class: Radical

Perhaps most distinctive, however, is the bodywork, all performed by Erickson himself. The frame was a joint effort between Thee Darkside of Daytona and Killer Choppers. Springer forks run at a steep rake of 68 degrees (most choppers are at 38-55 degrees), making for a huge turning radius. But then, it's doubtful Erickson ever intended this unique creation as an around-town grocery-getter.

Driver's-eye view reveals sculpted fuel tank topped by an extended fuel neck with spired cap.

Trop Chop

year: 2005
builder: Midwest Choppers
class: Radical

Chip Miyler of Midwest Choppers has earned a reputation for highly detailed, well-built choppers, and the Trop Chop is yet another testament to his many talents.

A stretched Midwest Choppers frame positions the neck two inches

up and five inches out, setting the extended American Suspension forks at a 48-degree rake. A rear swingarm with suspension by Progressive adds some comfort to the style.

Not willing to build an all-show, no-go chopper, Chip employed a 124-cubic-inch S&S engine for motivation. Matching Xtreme Machine rims host HHI disc brakes, and in back, a 280-mm tire.

But the real artistry of Trop Chop lies in the flowing bodywork and eye-catching paint scheme. Every inch of sheetmetal is of Chip's own creation, and the tropical scenes by Jeremy Imming detail underwater life in amazing imagery employing nearly every color of the spectrum. It all flows together to help cement Midwest Choppers' reputation as one of the country's premier builders.

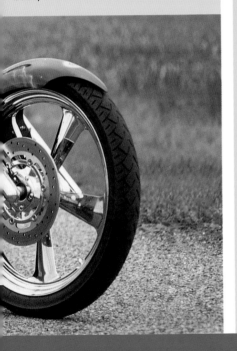

Turbo Spike

year: 2004
builder: Kaotic Customs
class: Radical

Based in Ft. Lauderdale, Florida, Kaotic Customs has designed and built numerous choppers for a variety of clients. No two have been alike, but a theme of high-quality fit and finish applies to every model sold.

As one might guess, Turbo Spike is powered by a boosted engine; in this case, a 100-cubic-inch S&S V-twin with Garrett turbocharger and exhaust plumbing bent by Kaotic Customs. The RC Components frame has been altered for the desired stance, with an air-adjustable triangulated swingarm in back and 14-inch-over inverted forks in front. Arlen Ness wheels with matching brake discs complete the chassis package. Topping it all off are bright red-and-yellow scorpion graphics on the sheetmetal, frame, and even the engine—a fitting paint scheme for a beautifully built chopper packing a turbocharged sting.

U-Bet 2

year: 2003
builder: Bill Steel
class: Radical

Hard to believe, but this radical chopper began life as a Harley-Davidson—albeit a wrecked one. Bill Steel was the artisan who transformed the pile of parts into the striking machine seen here.

Actually, about the only Harley components used were the 88-cubic-inch Twin Cam 88B engine and its attendant 5-speed transmission. The bent frame was replaced by a chassis from Goldammer, which included inverted forks in front and a single-sided RC Components swingarm in back. Both ends feature adjustable air suspension, the compressed air being stored in the frame tubes.

The fuel tank came from the catalog of Paul Yaffe, but was modified to blend into the surrounding custom sheetmetal. Both front and rear fenders, along with the oil-tank surround, were hand-formed by Bill Steel. RC Components supplied the wheels and the rear brake disc/pulley, which, along with the single-sided swingarm, allows the right side of the wheel to run completely free of obstruction.

Yes, it's hard to believe this grew out of a wreck. And it has certainly come a long way from Milwaukee....

Executioner

year: 2004
builder: Scooter Shooterz
class: Radical

Scooter Shooterz built the Executioner for the Discovery Channel's popular Biker Build-Off program. The honor of being asked to participate is matched only by the creativity of the chopper entered.

Assembled in just nine days, the Executioner bristles with little custom touches—along with one blazing big one: a "head" light that spews flames from its

Lest the description "spews flames from its gaping maw" had you thinking Zippo lighter or propane torch, think again. Got marshmallows?

gaping maw. Even without the fireworks, however, the bike is mighty impressive. Black paint carries gold-leaf accents, the rear fender is adorned with leather flames affixed with copper rivets, and the wheels were designed and cut by Scooter Shooterz itself.

The 107-cubic-inch engine features "Knucklehead"-style valve covers, a matte-black intake routed to the left side of the bike, and tape-wrapped exhaust. A pistol-grip hand shifter stirs the Baker 6-speed gearbox, leaving the clutch to be operated by a foot pedal. Legend air suspension allows the rider to adjust ride height at the rear, while Mean Street Warlord forks—featuring finely carved details—hold up the front.

But the highlight of the build is the flame-throwing, skull-shaped headlight. Lamps fill each eye socket, while the push of a button sends great waves of fire rolling from the open jaw. It certainly creates a spectacle, which is exactly what the Biker Build-Off program was all about.

Lethal Injection

The intricacies of the Hilborn injection system make the engine a work of art on its own. Note the elaborately sculpted fuel tank.

Scooter Shooterz has earned a reputation for building exotic choppers, but in terms of originality, Lethal Injection sets new standards. Proof of its allure came at a Louisville event, where it took Best Of Show honors.

At the heart of Lethal Injection is a 107-cubic-inch V-twin wearing 4-valve heads from Mega-Four and fed by a Hilborn mechanical fuel-injection system. Executed by Scooter Shooterz' own Warren Vesely, it performs even better than expected, overwhelming the massive 280-series rear tire under hard acceleration.

Oil for the engine is carried in the bike's frame downtube as well as externally mounted auxiliary storage tubes. Scooter Shooterz cut a pair of one-off wheels for Lethal Injection, and a GMA component does double duty as rear brake disc and drive pulley.

Every inch of the bodywork is original, and the fuel tank sets new standards for complexity. The chosen hue is Big Red Flake from the House Of Kolor, with silver-leaf accents and a seat embroidered with the bike's name adding custom touches to the high-powered beast.

Rock Hard

year: 2005
builder: Midwest Choppers/Rock Hymes
class: Radical

Rock Hymes wanted to build a unique chopper, but lacked some of the skills and tools required, so he approached Midwest Choppers about doing a cobuild. Rock had been impressed by the machines built by Midwest over the years, and the company was eager to be part of his team. Rock did some of the fabrication himself, drawing on Midwest's expertise when required.

The radical 51-degree rake joins with forks that are 24 inches over to throw the front end both up and out to nearly unprecedented proportions. Yet despite the extreme numbers, Rock Hard is easily ridden both on the highway and around town.

Power comes courtesy of a 124-cubic-inch S&S engine fitted with Vance & Hines exhaust and Midwest Choppers' trademark Maltese-cross air cleaner. Xtreme Machine rims roll at both ends, the rear being fitted with an enormous 300-series tire for ample traction.

Flame paint jobs are common, but not the type of "real" flame treatment given to Rock Hard. By using less-defined edging on the flames, they seem to roll and flow, much like the real thing.

Low Blow

year: 2003
builder: Thee Darkside of Daytona
class: Radical

Nearly anyone with the right amount of know-how can assemble a nice-looking chopper. But to build a bike of this complexity, do nearly all the work in-house, and complete the job in just a month takes a shop like Thee Darkside of Daytona.

What separates Low Blow from most other choppers can be summed up in one word: horsepower. Gobs of it. More than any sane person would ever need—or use. Beneath the skull-ringed fuel tank sits a 124-cubic-inch V-twin pressure fed by a roots-type supercharger. And if for some unfathomable reason that's not enough, extra boost is just a squirt of nitrous oxide away. All that power is transferred through a 5-speed gearbox with hand shifter. Slowing the bike down is the duty of Performance Machine disc brakes at both ends.

Interesting decorative touches are another trademark of Thee Darkside of Daytona machines. The hardtail frame features a distinctly styled rear section, while a spined backbone serves—worthlessly—as a rear fender. Forks ride at a radical 65-degree rake, which aids straightline stability when the horses stampede.

To think this all came together in a month's time is hard to imagine. But speedy work is Thee Darkside of Daytona's specialty—in more ways than one.

PRO STREET

year: 2005
builder: DD Custom Cycles
class: Pro Street

Dave Dupor of DD Custom Cycles is fast becoming one of the nation's hottest chopper builders. By combining the finest hardware with cutting-edge design and flawless workmanship, his machines are drawing the attention of buyers from across the country.

Many of today's choppers are lacking in the comfort and handling departments. But this one was built to satisfy the desire for a striking chopper that was also eminently drivable, and it rides as good as it looks.

The chassis consists of a swingarm frame from War Eagle hosting a set of Sunmyth forks. Added to that were full fenders that wrap around the tires, along with a fuel tank boasting subtle insets on both sides for a unique look.

Painted a two-tone scheme of Pearl Blue and Orient Blue, the colorful sheetmetal is closely matched by a set of blue-anodized Pro-One Sinister wheels. A diamond-cut finish on the 124-cubic-inch S&S engine adds even more sparkle to a machine that already draws its share of admiration.

CHECKERS

year: 1999
builder: Crown Custom Cycle Fabricatio[n]
class: Pro Street

Bud Dennis of Crown Custom Cycle Fabrications has a long-standing reputation for building high-performance Harley-Davidsons for the dragstrip. So it seems only natural he would eventually put his extraordinary knowledge to work on a street machine.

Though a Harley Softail model was the starting point, most major components have been replaced with more performance-oriented hardware. That includes the frame, purchased from Bourget Bike Works, needed to house the enlarged engine. Progressive supplied the rear suspension, but the original forks—shortened by two inches—hold up the front.

The heart of the beast is a hand-built 140-cubic-inch monster V-twin fed by twin S&S carburetors. And as if that weren't enough, there's also a nitrous oxide system onboard for added punch. Assigned to rein in all that power are dual Harley disc brakes in front and a single Performance Machine anchor in back.

Though "go" is certainly the name of the game here, "show" has not been ignored. An elaborate, brightly colored paint scheme combines with plenty of polished parts to turn heads as the bike goes by—most likely, very quickly.

SPEED DEMON

year: 2004
builder: DD Custom Cycles
class: Pro Street

Due to the high caliber of Dave Dupor's custom creations, clients often come back for a second helping. Such is the case with Speed Demon, as this is the second chopper Dave's DD Custom Cycles has built for the owner.

A stretched War Eagle frame with swingarm rear suspension holds 2-inch-over Mean Street telescopic forks. Weld Wheels are found at both ends, each holding a matching disc brake; in back, the disc rides inboard of the drive pulley. A Rivera 6-speed right-side-drive transmission and 124-cubic-inch S&S engine exhaling through Martin Bros. pipes complete the chassis picture.

A fuel tank stretched to match the elongated frame is joined by formed fenders and oil tank to achieve a custom look, and they're all covered in silver paint accented with an exotic flame motif. The end result is a custom chopper that may well bring its two-time owner back for more.

SUPERCHARGED

year: 2004
builder: Custom Shop Cycle
class: Pro Street

Once Custom Shop Cycles decided to build its first chopper, it went the route of full-blown crazy just to show the world what it could do. The company has since gone on to build many extreme machines, but this one still sets the pace.

Beginning with a Paramount Cycles hardtail frame, six inches were added to the backbone for a long, lean look. Pro-One forks hold a Weld wheel with HHI disc brake; in back, a matching rim is fitted with a GMA disc/pulley. A 280-mm tire puts power to the road.

And power this bike has—in spades. While a 113-cubic-inch engine is hardly extreme in today's chopper world, the addition of both a supercharger and nitrous oxide injection make a strong statement. So does the Hooker header when the ponies are cut loose.

Every inch of sheetmetal was formed by Custom Shop Cycles for this project, and over it, a multicolored paint scheme was applied. After all, if a bike is to serve as your mobile masthead, you wouldn't want it to be all "go" and no "show."

GLOSSARY

The world of choppers includes many words and terms that are not commonly used, or beg further explanation. Many of the following can be found in the text of this book, and often come up in any discussion of choppers.

Aftermarket companies: Producers of parts and accessories that are designed to fit on a production vehicle, but the companies don't make the vehicles themselves. These parts can include small items, like seats and mirrors, and also large ones, such as engines, transmissions, and even frames. Since many aftermarket chopper companies got their start supplying replacement parts for Harley-Davidson motorcycles, their products often resemble Harley components.

Ape hangers: Tall handlebars.

Billet: Solid chunks of metal—usually a lightweight aluminum alloy—that are cut and milled to form creative parts such as brake arms, footpegs, and mirror mounts.

Bobber: An early '50s-era custom motorcycle. One definition of "bob" is to cut shorter, and that's what customizers did to the full, heavy fenders fitted to most big bikes of the time. The idea was to save weight and give the machine a lean, purposeful look, and a bike so modified was said to be "bobbed," thus the name.

Brakes: Old-fashioned drum brakes are rare on choppers. Modern disc brakes have a large rotor that's gripped by a caliper; they work much the same way as hand brakes on a bicycle. Most motorcycles have the brake disc on one side of the rear wheel, the drive pulley (for

a belt) or sprocket (for a chain) on the other side. But on some choppers, the rear disc is either part of the pulley or sprocket, or is mounted inboard on the same side of the wheel. This leaves the other side of the wheel "open," providing onlookers a better view of it fancy design.

Diamond-cut: Serrations cut into the edges of the engine's cylinder fins to make them sparkle in the light.

Engines: Most are V-twins patterned after those offered by Harley-Davidson over the years. The are built by aftermarket companies (see entry) such as S&S, Rev Tech, TP Engineering, and Ultima, and are usually larger and much more powerful than Harley's engines, which are still used in many choppers. Aftermarket engines usually mimic the look of Harley's Evolution (more commonly called "Evo") V-twin built from 1984 to 1999, but others are made to look like the Harley-Davidson "Panhead" of 1948-65, or the "Shovelhead" of 1966-84. The nicknames Panhead, Shovelhead, and the earlier Knucklehead (1936 47) were all coined by riders—not Harley-Davidson—and referred to the look of the engines' valve covers.

Final drive: The belt or chain that transfers power from the transmission to the rear wheel.

Forks: They generally come in four styles. *Telescopic:* Lower "sleeves" slide up and down on tubes, compressing internal coil springs. *Inverted:* the same, only upside down; the sleeves are at the top. *Springer:* The wheel moves up and down on short arms; long rods connected to the arms activate coil springs at the top. *Girder:* Solid forks move up and down on short arms at the top, compressing a spring. In most cases, the length of extended forks is based on the length of standard Harley-Davidson Softail forks, so if they're "10 inches over," they're 10 inches longer than stock Harley forks.

Frames: They're offered by numerous companies, but their dimensions are based on a stock Harley-Davidson Softail frame. Oftentimes, the downtube in front of the engine has been lengthened or "stretched," as has the top tube (sometimes called the "backbone") above the engine. These alterations are often referred to as "up and out." So a frame that is "6 up, 5 out" has been stretched six inches "up" in the downtube, five inches "out" in the top tube. Some people use the term "down and back" (such as "6 down, 5 back") which means the same thing; they're just referring to stretch in the downtube and backbone.

Nitrous oxide: A gas that allows more fuel to be burned in the cylinders, resulting in more power. It is sometimes referred to as "laughing gas," as a purified form can be used as an anesthetic in surgery.

Primary drive: The belt or chain that transfers power from the engine to the transmission.

Rake: The angle of the forks, in degrees from vertical. The higher the number, the more the forks "stick out." The angle of the frame's neck determines most of the rake, but sometimes the triple trees (see entry) that hold the forks add even more rake.

Rear suspension: "Hardtail" choppers have no rear suspension. Others have conventional swingarms—either straight tubes, tubes bent into a design, or tubes that form a triangle—acting on coil springs that are usually concealed.

Stepped seat: Also known as a "King and Queen" seat, it positions the passenger high above the rider, and was a defining element of choppers from the '60s and '70s.

Tires: Most standard Harley-Davidsons come with rear tires that are 130-150 mm wide—about five to six inches. Some choppers have rear tires that are 300 mm wide (nearly the width of two pages of this book!), and recently, a company began offering a 360-mm tire.

Transmissions: Those built by aftermarket companies sometimes come with final-drive sprockets or pulleys on the right side rather than the normal left-side placement. This is usually done in order to accommodate a very wide rear tire. (See Tires.) Most are conventional foot-shift transmissions with a hand-operated clutch, but some—as noted in the text—are fitted with hand shifters and foot clutches, which were commonly used prior to the early 1950s.

Triple trees, or trees: Formed pieces that hold the fork legs, connecting them to the handlebars and frame neck. Some are designed to add more rake to the forks than is provided by the frame neck.

Wheels: Range from spoke-type that are relatively inexpensive, to one-off designs intricately milled from a solid disk of metal that can cost thousands of dollars apiece.

Photo on page 61 by Kristina Pamias. All other photographs by Doug Mitchel.

Very special thanks to the owners of the motorcycles pictured, without whose enthusiastic cooperation this book would not have been possible.